The Sullivan HERITAGE

Algernon Sydney Sullivan
Mary Mildred Sullivan &
George Hammond Sullivan

TRITON

Published by Triton Press, a division of The Nautilus Publishing Company
426 S. Lamar Blvd., #16, Oxford, MS 38655
Tel: 662-513-0159 • http://nautiluspublishing.com/

Dedicated to the Sullivan Foundations' Trustees Emeriti

Gray Williams, Jr, who served as a trustee from 1980 to 2009 following his father's retirement from the board. Gray was a valued trustee in all aspects, but particularly his invaluable service in writing the Sullivan Heritage book which follows.

Allan Strand served as trustee and the third president of the Foundation from 1994 to 2009. Through his vision and tireless work the Foundation moved from passively recognizing noble character to actively promoting service and social entrepreneurship among Sullivan students and communities.

ALGERNON SYDNEY SULLIVAN IN 1879

Introduction

In May, 1857, Algernon Sydney Sullivan and his wife, Mary Mildred, moved from Cincinnati, Ohio, to New York City to make a fresh start in life. He was 31 and she was 21. They had been married just a year and a half. They had very little money, since he had lost almost all his savings in the recession — then called a panic — that swept over the country the year before. They had virtually no friends or other connections in their new community.

The Sullivans spent the rest of their lives in New York. Algernon Sydney became a highly successful lawyer and a much-respected public citizen. He founded the law firm Sullivan and Cromwell, still pre-eminent today. Mary Mildred became a leader in New York society, renowned for her many charitable activities. Although their endeavors helped them establish a lasting home in New York, both had their roots in the South, particularly in Virginia, and they always remained faithful to their Southern heritage. Their son, George Hammond Sullivan, also shared their affection for the South, and he became largely responsible for keeping their memories alive.

Thus, when the Algernon Sydney Sullivan Foundation and the Algernon Sydney Sullivan and Mary Mildred Sullivan Awards were established, their primary mission was to support higher education in the South, with special attention to the often neglected region of Appalachia. The Sullivan Foundation now provides financial grants to 31 Southern schools and colleges, and oversees the Sullivan Awards that are offered at 67 such institutions.

The following biographies not only tell the story of the Sullivans against the background of the eventful times in which they lived, but also seek to explain their lasting impact on others. The idealism, personal magnetism, and strength of character of Algernon Sydney and Mary Mildred Sullivan endeared them to those who knew them during their lifetimes and provided the inspiration for the Sullivan Foundation and Sullivan Awards that are their lasting monuments.

Algernon Sydney Sullivan's
Family and Birth

Algernon Sydney Sullivan's father, Jeremiah Sullivan, was in turn the son of Irish and Scottish immigrants who made their home at Harrisonburg, in the Shenandoah Valley of Virginia. Jeremiah, born in 1794, was at once studious and enterprising. He attended William and Mary College, took time out to serve as an army officer during the War of 1812, and returned to graduate. He then "read law," as the custom was, with an attorney in Harrisonburg, and in 1816 was granted a license to practice in Virginia.

Not content to become a lawyer in his home town, Jeremiah harbored higher ambitions. He was attracted by reports of great opportunities in the states being carved out of the Northwest Territory west of the Appalachians, traveling first to Cincinnati in the new state of Ohio, and then further west down the Ohio River until he reached a small river port called Madison. It was located in the Territory of Indiana, which by the end of the year would itself become a state. He resolved to settle there, bought property, and contracted to have a substantial brick house built on it. Early in 1817, he returned to Virginia, where he persuaded his parents to join him at his new home. They packed up all their possessions, traveled by wagon to Pittsburgh, and floated down the Ohio on a flatboat to Madison, where the new house had been completed.

Jeremiah soon proved that his venturesome choice had been a wise one. His law practice throve and he became active in Indiana politics. In 1820 he served a term in the Indiana legislature, and was credited for devising a new, classically inspired name for the state capital – Indianapolis, or "Indiana City." From 1837 to 1846 he was Chief Justice of the state

Supreme Court, and a year before his death in 1870 was appointed a judge in the newly established Indiana Criminal Court.

He became an eminent citizen of his community as well. He was particularly active in the Presbyterian Church. He served as a Ruling Elder in his local congregation, and he was president of the Indiana Bible Society.

Just one year after settling in Madison, Jeremiah had prospered enough to marry. His bride was Charlotte Cutler, born in Richmond, Virginia, in 1798. They had eleven children. Their fourth child and second son was born on April 5, 1826, and christened Algernon Sydney.

JEREMIAH SULLIVAN, FATHER OF ALGERNON SYDNEY SULLIVAN
Born and raised in Virginia, Jeremiah Sullivan became a prominent attorney and statesman in Indiana.

Drawing by W. E. Mears

SULLIVAN FAMILY HOUSE IN MADISON, INDIANA
The home of Jeremiah and Charlotte Sullivan, where Algernon Sydney Sullivan
was born and grew up.

Who Was the Original
Algernon Sydney?

The name Algernon Sydney may now sound rather quaint, but it was not uncommon during the years around the American Revolution. Algernon Sydney (1623-1683), though born an aristocrat, was a prominent supporter of Oliver Cromwell in the rebellion against the absolutism of Charles I. He later turned against Cromwell, when the latter assumed dictatorial powers as Lord Protector. After the monarchy was restored under

Charles II, Sydney continued to defend republicanism and oppose tyranny of all kinds. He was executed for treason in 1683, more for his defiant political principles than for any proven acts. His *Discourses Concerning Government* became very influential as a justification for American independence, and Sydney was revered as a martyr for liberty. Among his admirers were both Thomas Jefferson and John Adams.

Algernon Sydney Sullivan was known as Algernon to his professional colleagues and other formal associates. Within his family, he was sometimes called Sydney, but never Al or Sid.

Algernon Sydney's Education

Jeremiah Sullivan was quite literate by the standards of his time, and he believed strongly in the value of education. There were no public schools in Indiana (nor in most other states) when Algernon Sydney was growing up, but his father saw to it that he had a very able tutor, British-born Roswell Elms. Like his father, Algernon Sydney was naturally studious, and readily absorbed Elms's instruction, which concentrated on literature, writing, and oratory in both English and Latin. This solid academic background served him well, professionally and personally, and he became a powerful advocate for education.

Two problems dogged Algernon Sydney Sullivan periodically throughout his life. First, his health was frail — he possessed low resistance to stress and infection. Second, his enormous mental energy sometimes outstripped his physical capacities, leading him to overexert himself to the point of collapse. These two problems tended to reinforce each other. Overwork provoked recurring bouts of sickness when he went to college, first at Hanover College, down the river from Madison, and then at Miami University, in Oxford, Ohio. Nevertheless, with characteristic determination he was able to complete his studies in just three years, graduating in 1845.

ALGERNON SYDNEY SULLIVAN IN 1849

This photograph, the earliest known portrait of Algernon Sydney Sullivan, was taken when he was 23 years old and starting to practice law in Cincinnati, Ohio.

A good part of Algernon Sydney's extreme conscientiousness arose from his profound admiration for his father. "My constant endeavor," he wrote while in college, "shall be, henceforth, to live worthy of such a father as my own, by practicing obedience to what I know to be duty, and particularly by exercising a prudent and cautious self-control."

It was not easy to "live worthy" of that father. Jeremiah Sullivan was an affectionate but exacting parent, who was not confident of his son's "prudent and cautious self-control." Even when Algernon Sydney was fully grown and an established attorney, Jeremiah wrote him letters with repeated warnings such as, "Let not *success* or *amusement* turn your thoughts away from God," and "Curb your *excitability* and your *impulsiveness*." The son hardly needed these admonitions – but he saved the letters.

Many years later, a friend and colleague, somewhat impatient with Algernon Sydney's unbending scrupulousness, asked, "Sullivan, have you ever been tempted to do anything which you thought was wrong?" After a pause, he replied, "Yes, frequently, but I always thought of my dear old father and then I could not do it."

A First Taste of Public Service

After his graduation from college, Algernon Sydney returned home to read law with his father, in preparation for following the same career. But in 1847, at the age of twenty, he took time off to get involved in public service. The year before, educational reformer Caleb Mills had begun a campaign to establish tax-financed public schools in Indiana. It was an uphill struggle – Americans have always been averse to taxes – but Algernon Sydney was determined to take part. For months he toured the state making speeches in favor of Mills's proposals. It was excellent training for a young lawyer, for he learned how to make persuasive arguments, counter opposition, and allay doubts. But he also found himself both naturally talented and well educated for public speaking in a period when outstanding orators were as popular as rock stars are today.

His efforts may have had a positive impact. In 1848 a majority of Indiana voters supported the concept of tax-supported education, setting in motion a process that would eventually result in a statewide system.

The Young Lawyer in Cincinnati

In 1849 Algernon Sydney completed his legal studies and received his license. Instead of remaining in Indiana and joining his father's practice, he decided to strike out and begin his career in the larger metropolis of Cincinnati, Ohio. In the fashion of the time, he rented a room to serve as both his office and his living quarters, and he painted his own "shingle," the sign that proclaimed his name and profession, to be mounted in his front window.

He established himself in his new community with surprising speed. His father's reputation may have helped some, but his agreeable looks and outgoing personality undoubtedly contributed. A photograph taken at the time, the first portrait we have of him, shows a handsome but still boyish face, with a broad forehead overhanging intense dark eyes.

He was by natural temperament a joiner. He became not only a member of the Second Presbyterian Church but an associate pastor. He served on the city school board, the Common Council, and as a director of the House of Refuge. A notable sign of his acceptance was an invitation, within a few months of his arrival, to join the Literary Club of Cincinnati, recently formed by a group of Cincinnati's intellectual elite. One of the other members was fellow lawyer Rutherford B. Hayes, who would later distinguish himself as an officer in the Civil War and eventually be elected U.S. President.

In late 1850, Algernon Sydney became engaged to Mary Slocum Groesbeck, who was much admired in Cincinnati society for both her beauty and sweet disposition. They married on January 2, 1851, but their happiness was cut short by her sudden death in September. Algernon Sydney managed his grief by devoting himself even more intensely to his work and public service.

For example, in December Cincinnati needed a delegate to speak at a gala reception in New York City in honor of the Hungarian patriot Louis Kossuth, who had come to the United States to seek support for his nation's independence. Algernon Sydney, already admired as an orator, accepted the assignment. His welcoming speech to Kossuth was well received. "May Hungary's awakening," he proclaimed in the effusive style favored at that time, "commence a new and happy epoch for the world – when the great bell of Time shall sound out another and a glad hour – the hour of jubilee and freedom. Then, Sir, the West will continue to unite her voice with the acclamation of all America, adopting your own fervent language, 'Hail! To Hungary, to her fame, her freedom, and her happiness.'"

A Political Shift and a Fortunate Meeting

As Algernon Sydney's legal practice continued to thrive, he began to take a more active role in politics. Like his father, he was originally a Whig, but that party fell apart as the country became increasingly divided over slavery. Some former Whigs joined the new Republican Party, devoted to opposing the extension of slavery into new states such as Kansas. But Algernon Sydney was instinctively a moderate and a conciliator, and his Southern sympathies ran deep. He felt that the Republicans were "too sectional" – they exclusively represented Northern views, and aroused nothing but antagonism in the South. He decided that the liberal wing of the Democratic Party, under leaders like Stephen A. Douglas, would better serve the interests of the country as a whole. In 1855, he lent his oratorical gifts to the Democratic campaign for Ohio governor, but Republican

Salmon P. Chase, later Secretary of the Treasury and Chief Justice, prevailed. The election was yet another step in the "irrepressible conflict" leading to the Civil War.

Also during 1855, a prominent Cincinnati merchant named Griffin Taylor received a visit by one of his in-laws from Virginia. George Washington Hammond was accompanied from Winchester by his eighteen-year-old daughter, who had recently finished school. Her name was Mary Mildred.

HAPPY RETREAT, NEAR CHARLES TOWN, VIRGINIA (NOW WEST VIRGINIA)
This pre-Revolutionary house was originally built by Charles Washington, a younger brother of George Washington. In 1836 it was the home of George Washington Hammond and Sarah Ann Hammond, and it was the birthplace of Mary Mildred Hammond.

Mary Mildred Hammond's Family and Early Childhood

Mary Mildred Hammond's parents, George Washington Hammond and Sarah Ann Taylor, were both descended from several generations of

Virginians, most of whom lived toward the northern end of the Shenandoah Valley. Mary Mildred was born November 3, 1836, at Happy Retreat, a pre-Revolutionary home that her father had inherited from his own parents. It was originally built by Charles Washington, a younger brother of the President, and was located near Charles Town, in what is now West Virginia. Mary Mildred was named after her father's youngest sister, who died the year before at age sixteen.

SHANNON HILL, NEAR CHARLES TOWN, VIRGINIA (NOW WEST VIRGINIA)
Built by Mary Mildred Hammond's father, George Washington Hammond, this was the home of the Hammond family from 1840 to 1844.

George Washington Hammond moved his family several times during Mary Mildred's childhood. Shortly after her birth, he sold his ancestral home and moved to a rented cottage while he built a larger house on land he had purchased elsewhere in the Charles Town area. Shannon Hill was completed by 1840, but the family remained there only four years. Mr. Hammond then decided to give up farming and to start up a general store in the larger center of Winchester, Virginia. He moved his family to hotels in Winchester while he completed his preparations.

THE HAMMOND CHILDREN IN 1847
Mary Mildred, shown standing at left, was the eldest. Next to her is Harriet (Hattie), and seated in front of them are William (Will) and the twins Tom and Henry.

BUSHROD TAYLOR, ABOUT 1838
A successful businessman in Winchester, Virginia, Bushrod Taylor was the husband
of Mary Mildred Hammond's great-aunt Betsey Taylor.

Shortly after settling into the first of these hotels, Mary Mildred had
a traumatic experience that in her own estimation had a profound and lasting impact upon her. An epidemic of scarlet fever struck Winchester, caus-
ing the schools to close. Mary Mildred's mother attempted to protect her
by forbidding her from leaving the hotel and its walled back garden, but
a child in the house next door died of the disease, and Mary Mildred became irresistibly curious to learn more about it. She climbed over the garden wall and briefly poked at some discarded bedding she found in the
adjacent yard. Soon, she came down with a mild case of scarlet fever, but

also infected her younger brother Will, three years old, who became desperately ill and nearly died. Mary Mildred was overwhelmed with guilt that her unthinking disobedience had caused so much harm to someone she loved.

In 1846, Mr. Hammond had opened his new store, and had finished renovating a house on Washington Street for his family. By this time, Mary Mildred was the eldest of five Hammond children, including a pair of twin boys. On September 17, 1846, her mother gave birth to another set of twins, a boy and a girl. It was a difficult birth, with tragic consequences. The boy died within a few hours, and the girl barely survived. Sarah Ann Taylor Hammond never recovered, and died on February 7, 1847, at the age of thirty.

Aunt Betsey Taylor

Upon the death of his wife, George Washington Hammond was left with six children, ranging in age from ten years to five months, while in the process of launching his business. He was fortunate to have help near at hand. Also living in Winchester were his wife's aunt, Elizabeth Milton Taylor, and her husband, Bushrod Taylor.

Bushrod Taylor, born in 1793, was a leading citizen of Winchester, and had made a success of several business ventures in the Shenandoah Valley. Elizabeth Milton, familiarly known as Betsey, fell in love with him the first time she saw him. They married in 1817, when she was not quite seventeen. Undoubtedly they both wanted children, but never had any of their own. Betsey Taylor more than made up for that lack.

Ever since her marriage, Betsey had become a close friend of Bushrod's sister, Harriot Taylor Ware. Both Harriot and John Ware suffered from tuberculosis, and not many years after Bushrod and Betsey were married, the Wares fell mortally ill. Before her death, Harriot appealed to Betsey to care for her four children, and without hesitation Betsey agreed.

BETSEY MILTON TAYLOR, ABOUT 1838
The wife of Bushrod Taylor, she served as the foster mother both of her niece Sarah Ann Hammond and of her great-niece Mary Mildred Hammond.

Such arrangements were not uncommon in an era when lives could be precarious and short. When both parents died, their children would customarily be sent to live with relatives or friends, and the orphans would be lucky if they were not separated from one another. Moreover, since women bore the primary responsibility for raising children, a mother's death might compel the father to place the children in the care of other women.

Harriot Ware may have foreseen that her sister-in-law and close friend

Betsey Taylor would prove exceptionally well suited for the task. The children's health was frail. The youngest daughter died a few months after her parents. The two boys died of tuberculosis in childhood, and only the eldest daughter survived to become an adult. Betsey loved and cared for them all, and grieved over those who died, as if they were her own.

In 1824, Bushrod and Betsey Taylor took in two more children. Bushrod's older brother William was married to Betsey's younger sister Harriot. An epidemic of typhoid fever caused Harriot's untimely death, and William arranged to have Betsey take charge of his two daughters, Florinda, age four, and Sarah Ann, age seven. Sarah Ann Taylor would grow up to become the wife of George Washington Hammond and the mother of Mary Mildred Hammond.

Florinda and Sarah Ann were lucky. Their father remarried two years later and was able to bring his family together again. But Sarah Ann remained close to her Aunt Betsey and her cousin Catherine Ware for the rest of her life.

When Sarah Ann died in 1847, it was quite natural for George Washington Hammond to look once again to Aunt Betsey for help. Mary Mildred and her brothers and sisters all went to live at Aspen Hill, the Taylor farm on the outskirts of Winchester. Mary Mildred regarded Betsey as her second mother, and this wise and generous woman in turn had a deep and lasting influence on her great-niece.

Within six months, tragedy again struck the family and added still further to Betsey Taylor's responsibilities. Bushrod Taylor underwent what was supposed to be a minor operation on his foot, but the wound became infected and the infection spread. He died on July 14, 1847, at the age of 54. In her bereavement, Betsey not only continued to manage a large household, but also settled and consolidated Bushrod's wide-ranging business affairs. George Washington Hammond himself moved to Aspen Hill at this time, in order to remain close to his children and presumably to assist Betsey as well, but he was very much preoccupied with his own enterprise.

MARY MILDRED HAMMOND IN 1855
At the time of their marriage, Mary Mildred Hammond was 19 years old
and had finished school just one year earlier.

Mary Mildred Grows Up

Mary Mildred Hammond was just ten years old when her mother died. Like many first children, she felt a deep sense of responsibility for her younger brothers and sisters, and her loyalty to her family always remained a crucial part of her life. She was serious-minded and curious, an enthusiastic student and a voracious reader. By nature, by upbringing, and by the vicissitudes of her early life, she became an adult by the time she had finished school at age 18 and was mature beyond her years.

ALGERNON SYDNEY SULLIVAN IN 1855
Algernon Sydney Sullivan was 29 years old and was already an established lawyer
in Cincinnati.

But she was a vivacious and attractive young woman as well, with broad, open features, intense black eyes, and luxuriant dark hair. Her father enjoyed her company, and in her late teens he would take her along on some of his business trips. The first of these was a memorable visit to New York City in 1853, where they attended the World's Fair at the spectacular Crystal Palace. At the time, Mary Mildred had no idea that New York would later become her home for the greater part of her life.

In 1855, Mr. Hammond took Mary Mildred with him to Cincinnati, where he visited Bushrod Taylor's brother Griffin Taylor. There she was introduced to a rising young attorney named Algernon Sydney Sullivan. They took to each other right away.

Later that year, Algernon Sydney, accompanied by his mother and sisters, traveled for a stay at the spa of White Sulphur Springs, in what is now West Virginia. Winchester, Virginia, was not far away, and Algernon Sydney took the opportunity to go and see Mary Mildred. They became engaged. Both families enthusiastically supported the match, in part because the two of them were so obviously fond of each other, and in part because they shared so much of the same heritage.

Early Years of Marriage, Cincinnati and New York

Algernon Sydney Sullivan and Mary Mildred Hammond married on December 13, 1855, at Aspen Hill. It was unseasonably warm that fall in Virginia, and chrysanthemums and even roses were still in bloom. The groom was 29, the bride just 19. After a short wedding trip, as honeymoons were then called, they settled back in Cincinnati, and Algernon Sydney's law practice continued to prosper.

Within a year, however, they suffered financial disaster. By the end of 1856, a period of economic buoyancy and widespread speculation ended in an inevitable crash. Algernon Sydney was not himself in debt, but the custom of the time, together with his own generous and trusting temperament, impelled him to co-sign the promissory notes of several of his friends. When they failed, he became responsible for their debts.

His savings and investments were wiped out, and he was forced to sell his treasured library, yet he still couldn't satisfy all his creditors. He concluded that he could no longer stay in Cincinnati. He didn't run out on his debts – indeed, he spent many years in fully repaying them. But in May, 1857, he and Mary Mildred resettled in what was the largest and most dynamic city in the country, New York.

ASPEN HILL, WINCHESTER, VIRGINIA
Algernon Sydney Sullivan and Mary Mildred Hammond were married at Bushrod and
Betsey Taylor's farm on the outskirts of Winchester. It had become the home of Mary
Mildred and her siblings after the death of their mother in 1847.

Like many city residents, the Sullivans avoided the expense and in-
convenience of setting up a separate and independent household. Instead,
they moved into a boarding house — Mrs. Coit's, at the corner of Ninth
Street and University Place. Algernon Sydney had brought with him letters
of introduction from colleagues and friends in Cincinnati, but only one of
these proved immediately valuable. Daniel Lord, Jr., of the firm of Lord,
Day, and Lord, was impressed by the young attorney from Ohio, and sponsored him for admission to the New York State Bar, a necessary prerequi-
site for practice there.

Algernon Sydney nonetheless chose not to associate himself with any
existing partnership. He "hung out his shingle" in a small office of his own
on William Street near the Wall Street financial center. Through his personal and professional connections, he was able to establish a practice

largely based on representing clients from the South and West. It was a moderate success and enabled the Sullivans to make a fresh start in their new and unfamiliar environment.

At the same time, Algernon Sydney and Mary Mildred did their best to turn the unfamiliar into the familiar by making friends and becoming active in the community. They joined the congregation of the Brick Presbyterian Church, then located at Fifth Avenue and 37th Street. Algernon Sydney became superintendent of the Sunday school and often offered his talents as an inspirational speaker at the Five Points Mission in the poorest and most notorious slum of the city.

Moving the Remains of James Monroe

A year after his arrival in New York, Algernon Sydney helped solidify his growing reputation by a characteristically unselfish act of public service. In early 1858, he attended a convention of the Sons of the Old Dominion, an association of businessmen and professionals who originally came from Virginia. One of the matters discussed at the meeting was a project dear to the members' hearts. When former President James Monroe had died in New York in 1831, his body was buried in the New York City Marble Cemetery on East Second Street. As the centennial of his birth approached, the State of Virginia, led by Governor Henry Wise, offered to have his remains returned to his native state. The Sons of the Old Dominion agreed to handle the arrangements in New York and formed a committee to carry out the task. Jeremiah Sullivan had been a personal friend of Monroe's, so it was quite natural for Algernon Sydney to volunteer as secretary of the committee.

He soon found himself responsible for all the many logistical details involved. The removal from the Marble Cemetery on July 2 became a major public celebration, with a parade at which Virginia-born General Winfield Scott was the grand marshal. The elite New York Seventh Militia

Regiment served as the guard of honor and accompanied the body as it traveled by ship to Richmond, where elaborate ceremonies awaited at Hollywood Cemetery. Algernon Sydney was proud of his role. He later commented to a friend, "I had at last done something worthy of my own honored father and of the great and good old President James Monroe."

BETSEY TAYLOR AND GEORGE HAMMOND SULLIVAN IN 1860
May Mildred Sullivan's beloved great-aunt Betsey came north to visit the Sullivans about a year after the birth of their son. In 1862, she was able to move from Virginia to New York, where she remained until the end of the Civil War.

Birth of George Hammond Sullivan

By 1859, Algernon Sydney and Mary Mildred had moved to another boarding house, Mrs. Howland's on West 14th Street. On November 21, 1859, Mary Mildred gave birth to the couple's only child, George Hammond Sullivan, named after her father.

Soon after, Mary Mildred's beloved great-aunt Betsey Taylor came north to visit the Sullivans to provide assistance to the young mother. A contemporary photograph shows baby George settled comfortably in Aunt Betsey's lap.

The Outbreak of War

The secession of Virginia on April 7, 1861, following the attack on Fort Sumter and Lincoln's call for volunteers to suppress the rebellion, produced a crisis for the Sullivan family. Algernon Sydney was torn in his sentiments. He was personally opposed to slavery and favored gradual emancipation as the best long-term policy for the nation. He also believed that the Union ought to be preserved, and that the Southern states were unwise to secede. At the same time, he thought that individual states did have the right to secede, just as the American colonies had exercised the right to become independent from England, to defend their liberty against tyranny. As a peacemaker, he deplored the use of military force to resolve the conflict.

His political stance was shared by many in New York. The city was sharply divided between Republicans, most of whom pressed for immediate attack upon the seceding states, and Democrats, who tended to favor compromise over war. The Democratic Party represented the majority and was in firm political control. Many in the business and professional classes, like Algernon Sydney, had close ties with peers in the South. Also, Democratic machine politicians such as William Marcy "Boss" Tweed held sway over the poor and working classes by fanning their fear of competition from black freedmen. Later in the war, that venal strategy would bring horrific consequences.

There were no such ambiguities in Mary Mildred's views. Family loyalty was far more important than politics. Two of her brothers, Will and

Tom Hammond, as well as two of her cousins, Willie and Tom Burnett, joined the Confederate armed forces. Family homes lay in the path of the contending armies. From the beginning of the war, Mary Mildred was determined to help her relatives in any way she could.

Defense of the Crew of the *Savannah*

Two months after the fall of Sumter, events led to the greatest personal ordeal Algernon Sydney ever had to endure. On June 4, the armed schooner *Savannah*, sailing out of Charleston, South Carolina, captured the merchant brig *Joseph*, owned by citizens of Maine and carrying a cargo of sugar from the West Indies. Captain Thomas H. Baker of the *Savannah* was flying the flag of the newly formed Confederate States of America, and carried a so-called "letter of marque" from that government. Letters of marque were a legal device that permitted privately owned ships to operate as armed privateers, licensed to take enemy vessels as prizes of war.

In accordance with the letter of marque, a small prize crew sailed the *Joseph* and its own crew back to Charleston, to be turned over to Confederate authorities. Later that same day, the *Savannah* attacked another ship, thinking it was also a merchant vessel. It was instead the United States Navy brig-of-war *Perry*, which quickly forced the smaller, lightly armed schooner to surrender. Captain Parrott of the *Perry* put Captain Baker and his twelve crew members in irons and sailed to New York. There all thirteen were jailed in the city's Tombs prison and charged with piracy. If convicted, they would be hanged.

The Lincoln administration didn't want to recognize the Confederate States as a separate, legitimate government. In particular, it refused to accept the Confederacy's right to issue letters of marque to privateers, even if they flew the Confederate flag and their officers wore Confederate uniforms. That is why the crew of the *Savannah* were treated as criminals rather than prisoners of war. But many people, in the North as well as the

South, believed that this policy was cruelly unjust. Among them was Algernon Sydney Sullivan. He agreed to join a team of lawyers, including his friend Daniel Lord, who were commissioned by the Confederacy to defend the alleged pirates.

FORT LAFAYETTE IN 1861 *(Drawing by W.E. Mears)*
This dank island fortress was built atop a shoal in the Narrows of New York Harbor.
Here Algernon Sydney Sullivan was held on suspicion of treason, but without formal
charges, for seven weeks in the fall of 1861. The rocky shoal now anchors one of the
stanchions of the Verrazano Bridge.

For reasons that are not entirely clear, the Lincoln administration concentrated its hostility upon Algernon Sydney. Perhaps he came under suspicion because of his known connections with clients in the South, or because of the letters he wrote to Confederate authorities requesting documents to support the defense. The real motivation may have been simply to intimidate the defense team. In any event, on September 11, Secretary of State William Seward ordered Algernon Sydney's arrest for "treasonous correspondence" with the enemy. He was not formally charged, but he was held in Federal custody at Fort Lafayette, a dank fortress on a shoal in the Narrows of New York Harbor. (The rocky shoal now anchors one of the stanchions of the Verrazano Bridge.)

Algernon Sydney remained at Fort Lafayette for seven weeks. Mary Mildred tried repeatedly to see him, but was allowed only one brief visit. He was finally released after taking an oath of allegiance to the Union, just two days before the trial of the *Savannah* crew was scheduled to begin.

Daniel Lord and the other defense attorneys tried to persuade Algernon Sydney to withdraw for fear that he might face further attack by the Government or even assassination by Union extremists. He refused. "If my clients do not desire to avail themselves of my services, they can excuse me," he told Lord. "But if they insist on my representing them, I as a man and as a lawyer must stand and do my duty."

The trial began on October 21 and lasted eight days. Along with other members of the team, Algernon Sydney offered a spirited defense, based on the precedent of the American Revolution: "Remember that you are an American jury; that your fathers were revolutionists; that they judged for themselves what Government they would have; and that they did not hesitate to break off from their other Government....By a conviction of the defendants, you condemn the Revolution of your ancestors....As you love the honor of your country, and her place among nations, refuse to pronounce these men pirates."

Justice Samuel Nelson might have directed a guilty verdict, based on the authority of Federal law, but he left the issue up to the jury to decide.

The jury failed to agree on a verdict, reflecting the deep political divisions among New Yorkers over the war.

Meanwhile, the Confederate government threatened to retaliate. It published the names of prisoners of war who would be executed if any of the *Savannah* crew members were so punished. The Lincoln administration concluded that even if the Confederacy was not formally recognized, its claims as a belligerent had to be honored. The prosecution was dropped. Captain Baker and his crew were transferred from the Tombs to Fort Lafayette as prisoners of war and were later exchanged. No further action was taken against any of those involved in their defense.

MARY MILDRED SULLIVAN IN 1862

Mary Mildred never concealed her loyalty to her family or her Southern sympathies. She corresponded with Confederate prisoners of war and endeavored to make their conditions easier. Later in the war, she would even travel to Virginia to assist her relatives.

Algernon Sydney remained deeply wounded by the injustice that had been inflicted upon him and never completely recovered from it. He suffered physically as well. Never in robust health, he contracted dysentery from polluted drinking water at Fort Lafayette, and its debilitating effects lingered for many years afterward.

After the *Savannah* trial, Algernon Sydney maintained a low public profile throughout the war and took part in no other controversial cases. Mary Mildred was careful not to compromise her husband with any act that might be construed as openly disloyal. But she did not conceal her Southern sympathies. She managed to get occasional letters through the lines to her relatives in Virginia, and she corresponded regularly with Confederate prisoners of war in the North, offering comfort and spiritual support without espousing their cause. Through 1862 she helped run a soup kitchen for the prisoners of war interned at David's Island in Long Island Sound off the coast of New Rochelle. Brigadier General Edward Canby eventually closed the soup kitchen and refused to renew Mary Mildred's permit to visit the prisoners, pronouncing her to be "a dangerous woman."

The Draft Riots of 1863

By the spring of 1863, the armed forces of the Union were in desperate need of more recruits. As the war dragged on and casualties mounted, volunteers became steadily scarcer. In March, the Lincoln administration persuaded Congress to pass a law authorizing a draft among all able-bodied men aged 21 to 35, and unmarried men up to 45, to be selected by lot.

The law was unpopular, particularly in New York City, where enthusiasm for the war had never been strong. And no one resented the law more than Irish immigrants, who made up about a quarter of the population. Most of them were poor, for usually only the lowest-paying jobs were open to them. They were especially galled by one important exception contained in the law – anyone drafted could escape service by a payment of $300. This confirmed their suspicion that the Union cause was "a rich man's war, but a poor man's fight."

Accompanying resentment of the draft was deep hostility of poor whites towards blacks. They feared the competition from black workers for the more menial jobs in the city. After Lincoln's Emancipation Proclamation, they imagined that a flood of black freedmen would overwhelm the city, taking away their jobs or driving down their wages. They were further inflamed by Democratic politicians, who convinced them that the Republicans favored blacks at their expense.

The Lincoln administration delayed putting the draft law into effect. Federal agents spent May and June collecting the names of eligible men, and the drawings were held off in hopes of encouraging news from the battlefronts. That news came on July 4, with the announcement of the two crucial victories at Gettysburg and Vicksburg, but resentment of the draft among poor whites in New York City continued to seethe.

The first drawing of draftees' names took place on Saturday, July 11, at one of the Federal provost marshal general's offices, at 3rd Avenue and 46th Street. It went smoothly. A second drawing was scheduled for the following Monday at the same office.

Early Monday morning, July 13, thousands of rioters boiled out of the slums in lower Manhattan and surged through the city. One of their first targets was the draft office. The second drawing had scarcely begun when they smashed open the building and set it on fire. They also attacked other government buildings, as well as the homes and businesses of the wealthy, particularly Republicans. Horace Greeley's *New-York Tribune*, for example, had to withstand a two-day siege. Many of the white rioters also sought out black men for beatings and lynchings.

One of the most shameful episodes occurred Monday afternoon, when rioters looted and burned the Colored Orphan Asylum at 5th Avenue and 43rd Street. Fortunately, the children, though terrified, were safely evacuated beforehand. But the rioters exulted in the destruction of what was, to them, a hateful symbol of Republican paternalism. That afternoon they continued to rage through the affluent neighborhood, searching for the homes of Republicans – or those they believed to be Republicans.

BURNING OF THE NEW YORK COLORED ORPHANS ASYLUM, JULY 13,1863
On the first day of the draft riots, a mob looted and burned the home for black orphans.
Fortunately the children were led to safety at the beginning of the attack.
(New York Public Library Picture Collection)

One of the largest of these homes belonged to Dr. Thomas Ward, at 5th Avenue and 47th Street. According to a Sullivan family legend, the mob tore apart the iron fence and used the bars as clubs.Then they threatened to burn down the house. Dr. Ward's niece slipped out the back door and ran for help from Mr. Sullivan on 45th Street. Algernon Sydney is reported to have made his way to the Wards' front porch, where he employed calm eloquence to persuade the rioters to retire.

This story was corroborated by John Torrey, a professor at Columbia College, which at that time was located a few blocks away at 50th Street and Madison Avenue. In a letter he wrote to a Harvard colleague that evening, Torrey reported that a mob had indeed threatened the Ward home. According to his account, the family had successfully convinced the rioters that the Wards were Peace Democrats rather than Republicans, and that Dr. Ward had voted for John Breckinridge for President rather than for Lincoln. Such arguments might have been persuasive, and it is not implausible that Algernon Sydney Sullivan might have served as the Wards' advocate. After all, he was a Peace Democrat. In any event, the family afterwards regarded Algernon Sydney as their savior.

The riots were finally suppressed a few days later with the aid of Federal troops, and New York returned to normal. A few weeks later, to the Sullivans' great relief, Mary Mildred's great-aunt Betsey Taylor was able to leave Virginia for safety in the North. She brought with her Mary Mildred's youngest sister, Florinda, and a four-year old cousin, Ned Stribling, whose mother had died a few months earlier. The Sullivans found them a house to rent, at 165 West 34th Street, and they settled there until the end of the war.

Ned Stribling and George Sullivan were the same age and became close friends for the duration of their lives. Florinda Hammond married New Yorker John Tilford in 1869 and continued to live in the North for many years. Betsey Taylor returned to the South after the war, but came back to New York for frequent, extended visits. She was living with the Sullivans when she died in 1883, at the age of 82.

Mary Mildred Travels to the South

In the summer of 1864, Mary Mildred received devastating news. Her beloved brother Will Hammond had died on July 4, after being severely wounded six days earlier in a skirmish at Stony Creek, south of Petersburg, Virginia. Will had joined a Confederate cavalry unit right at the beginning of the war and fought in many major battles. He had been wounded twice before. He was the second member of Mary Mildred's family to be lost to the war. Two years earlier, her cousin Tom Burnett died of an infectious disease contracted while in the army. Sickness, in fact, killed more Civil War soldiers than combat did.

MARY MILDRED'S BROTHER WILLIAM HAMMOND, DIED JULY 4, 1864
A Confederate cavalry officer, Mary Mildred's younger brother Will died of wounds suffered in a skirmish near Petersburg, Virginia. He was 23 years old.

After Will's death, Mary Mildred became determined to visit her beleaguered family in the South and to bring them whatever help she could. She had two main destinations. The first was Burnley, the home of her father's sister Ann Burnett, near Charles Town. The second was Springsberry, the home of her father's stepmother, Hannah Taylor, near Berryville.

They were no longer in the same state. When Virginia seceded from the Union in 1861, 48 of its northern and western counties in turn seceded from Virginia and, in 1863, became the new state of West Virginia. Charles Town, in Jefferson County, became part of West Virginia, and Berryville, in Clarke County, remained within Virginia. During the war, the whole area was heavily fought over and changed hands several times. So, travel to either Burnley or Springsberry was difficult and dangerous.

Mary Mildred packed two trunks full of clothes and portable household items that her relatives were likely to need. She decided that the best way to avoid interference from Yankee soldiers was to pass herself off as a harmless local farm woman. She dressed in plain clothes and took four-year-old George and a maid along with her. At the border between Maryland and West Virginia, they transferred the contents of the trunks to rough sacks and hired a horse and wagon to make their way to Charles Town.

They arrived safely at Burnley, where they stayed a few days. Aunt Ann had been a widow for many years and was managing the farm with little help. In 1862, Burnley had been occupied and looted by Union soldiers, and she had been forced to move temporarily to Winchester. She was able to return, however, and Burnley was not much harmed thereafter, despite Ann's evident Southern sympathies and the fact that her surviving son, Willie Burnett, was serving in the Confederate army.

The journey across the border into Virginia was longer and more hazardous, but Mary Mildred and her companions again managed to escape challenge. They stayed for some months at Springsberry, where Grandma Taylor, then 68, was living with her daughter-in-law, Gertrude McGuire, and Mary Mildred's sister Hattie.

The fertile Shenandoah Valley was the chief source of food and forage for Robert E. Lee's Army of Northern Virginia. In the autumn of 1864, Union General Philip Sheridan was conducting a scorched-earth campaign through the Valley, designed to deprive the Confederates of these vital supplies. Many farms were pillaged and burned, and during Mary Mildred's visit, Springsberry escaped destruction at least twice.

The first raid occurred early one morning while the family was having breakfast. Union soldiers surrounded the house and began to round up the remaining cows. Inside, Mary Mildred was able to scoop the silverware off the table and hide it on top of a tall wardrobe, where it lay forgotten and wasn't rediscovered until the next spring cleaning. Without explanation, the invaders departed in a hurry. They left the cows behind, but they did set fire to a stack of unthreshed wheat, which the family was counting on to sustain them through the winter. There were no men on the place, but Mary Mildred seized a pitchfork and raked off the burning straw, saving most of the grain. The charred pitchfork at Springsberry became a treasured family relic.

Shortly afterward, Sheridan's forces again swept through the area. Mary Mildred and her relatives feared that the house would be destroyed, and they removed from it as much furniture and as many personal possessions as they could. But even as they observed the red glow of their neighbors' burning homes, their own was passed by.

By mid-November, Mary Mildred returned North with George and her maid. Her rustic disguise was effective, and they passed through the Union-occupied countryside without ever being stopped or questioned.

The Execution of John Y. Beall

Back at home in early 1865, as the war was nearing its end, Mary Mildred became involved in the cause of a noted Confederate prisoner. John Yates Beall was the son of family friends in Charles Town. An ardent supporter of secession, he served in the Confederate army and navy, but by the fall of 1864 he was in Canada, making clandestine attacks on targets in upstate New York. In December, he was starting an operation to derail trains carrying Confederate prisoners, so that they might escape, when he was arrested at Niagara Falls. He was transferred to New York City and was tried the following January in a military court. Convicted as a spy, he was sentenced to be hanged.

JOHN YATES BEALL

In early 1865, as the war was nearing its end, John Y. Beall was captured while leading guerrilla raids in northern New York. He was convicted as a spy and sentenced to hang. Mary Mildred managed to visit him and to arrange a final meeting with his mother before his execution.

Great efforts were made to gain him a pardon, including personal appeals to Lincoln and a petition signed by 92 members of Congress. Lincoln, however, delegated the decision to the military commander in New York, General John A. Dix. Lincoln knew full well what that decision would be. Dix was an upright but implacable War Democrat, who was determined that Beall should be executed.

When Mary Mildred learned of Beall's conviction and realized their connection, she began trying to visit him on behalf of his family. It took several trips to the office of crusty General Dix before he would grant her a pass. On February 16, she was finally able to cross New York Harbor from Brooklyn to Governor's Island, where Beall was imprisoned at Fort Columbus. He welcomed her gratefully. He entrusted her with instructions for the trusteeship of his estate, and gave her a photograph to be copied for his family and friends. He also provided her with a lock of his hair, strands of which were to be braided into pieces of mourning jewelry, in accordance with the custom of the time.

Following her visit, Mary Mildred was able to accomplish something even more meaningful. She persuaded General Dix to allow Beall's mother a final reunion before his execution.

John Y. Beall was hanged at Fort Columbus on February 24. A few of his friends were permitted to attend. His final words were, "Bury me here, and take me not to the Valley, until my mother can write upon my tomb – 'He died in the defense of his country.'"

The Post-war Years

The end of the Civil War not only brought peace to the country but also relieved many of the anxieties that the Sullivans had endured during the conflict. Mary Mildred, in particular, no longer needed to be fearful for the safety of her family. When great-aunt Betsey Taylor left New York for Virginia in the fall of 1865, she established a new household in Berryville, not far from the Taylor family homestead of Springsberry. There she made a home for Mary Mildred's sisters, Hattie and Flo, and for great-nephew Ned Stribling. Mary Mildred brought down furniture from New York and helped them set up housekeeping.

An ongoing concern, however, was the uncertain health of young George. Like his father, George was subject to frequent infections and other illnesses. One popular tactic for improving the health of city children was to send them out into the more salubrious atmosphere of the country, especially during the summer. The Sullivans started sending George to spend summers in the South in 1866. He stayed with his great-aunt Ann Burnett at Burnley, near Charles Town, West Virginia, and also visited his relatives at Berryville. Although he was only six, he enjoyed his first stay away from home, learning to fish and ride, and playing with his cousin Ned.

GEORGE SULLIVAN IN 1869
While living with Betsey Taylor in Berryville, Virginia, when he was nine years old, George sent his parents this photograph of himself in country clothes and bare feet.

George was seriously ill in the winter of 1868 to 1869, contracting both measles and mumps and a series of respiratory and stomach disorders. In April 1869, his parents decided to send him south for a longer period. He lived with his great-great aunt Betsy for more than a year and attended a school run by his aunt Hattie. He was initially enthusiastic, and sent home a photograph of himself in casual clothes and bare feet – one of the pleasures enjoyed by a boy in the country. As the months passed, though, he grew increasingly homesick. As he reported in his letters, he missed his parents and his dog, a black-and-tan terrier named Spry.

George's health improved after 1870, and he returned to spending only summers in Virginia and West Virginia. But his stays there instilled in him his mother's deep love for the South, in particular the beauty of the countryside and the warmth of close family relationships.

In the years following the war, Algernon Sydney rebuilt his practice. He was able to restore some of his contacts with Southern businessmen and professionals, and he reinforced his already strong reputation for fairness, eloquence, scrupulous honesty, and unflagging devotion to his clients.

Naturally outgoing and generous, he went out of his way to befriend many of the young men who migrated from the South to seek greater opportunities in New York after the war. He and Mary Mildred made a custom on Sunday evenings of being "at home" for such newcomers, serving "high tea" (really a light supper) and providing entertainment such as hymn singing and discussions of politics, art, and literature.

Meanwhile, Mary Mildred was becoming deeply involved in charity work. Her first project was a natural for her. In 1866 she joined six other women in forming a temporary organization, the New York Ladies Relief Association, devoted to raising money for Southern women and children left destitute by the war.

Soliciting for this cause in postwar New York City wasn't easy. "Not one cent!" exclaimed one Canal Street merchant whom Mary Mildred approached. "They are rebels and they ought to starve!" Nonetheless, the association managed to collect at least $20,000 – a significant sum in those days – to be distributed by clergy in the Southern states.

Later that year, one of the other members of the association, Mrs. Henry Acton, recruited Mary Mildred to serve on the board of one of New York's major charities, the Nursery and Child's Hospital. This pioneering organization provided a wide range of services to poor women and children. It operated a maternity and pediatric hospital, day-care center, and orphanage in Manhattan, and also a satellite center in what was then rural Staten Island. One of its main sources of support was an annual Charity Ball, perhaps the most important event of the city's social season. The ball took place every February in a large central hall such as the Metropolitan Opera, and was thronged with the city's most affluent and prominent citizens. Mary Mildred quickly became one of its most active trustees and would later rise to be its leader.

16 WEST 11TH STREET
Purchased by Algernon Sydney in 1870, this classic New York City brownstone would become the home of himself and Mary Mildred for the rest of their lives, and the home of their son, George, for his lifetime as well.
(Drawing by W.E. Mears)

Five years after the end of the war, Algernon Sydney's practice had prospered enough to make a significant change in their way of life. Ever since they moved to New York in the 1850s, the Sullivans had lived in a series of boardinghouses and rented quarters. In 1870, Algernon Sydney bought them a house of their own, a classic New York "brownstone" at 16 West 11th Street. It would be their home for the rest of their lives, and the home of their son, George, for his lifetime as well.

Algernon Sydney and Democratic Reform

In the years after the Civil War, the Democratic Party suffered nationally for its association with the Southern rebellion. In New York City, however, the Democratic machine led by William Marcy ("Boss") Tweed consolidated its control. Its power was based on a system of small favors and patronage jobs handed out to its supporters to assure their votes, and it was largely financed by bribes and kickbacks on corrupt government contracts, funneled to Tweed and his Tammany Hall cronies. It enjoyed the loyalty of the poor and low-level working classes, and by the end of the 1860s Tweed's reign seemed to be unassailable.

At the same time, Reform Democrats in the city and state, under leaders such as Samuel J. Tilden, were attempting to bring some measure of honesty to New York politics. Their efforts were usually in vain, but once in awhile, they were able to obtain a government office for one of their supporters. In 1870, they managed to have Algernon Sydney Sullivan appointed an Assistant Attorney General for New York City.

To take this position required sacrifice by Algernon Sydney, for his own practice was more rewarding. He might have been well compensated by the bribes so widely available to government officials, but he was incorruptible. He tackled the job of enforcing the law and defending the legitimate interests of the city with his customary zeal and won widespread respect for his integrity — and his legal talents.

That same year a disgruntled former city employee leaked to the *New York Times* secret financial records that revealed the enormous extent of the Tweed administration's corruption. The scandal unleashed concentrated attacks in the press. Some of the most effective of these were the trenchant cartoons of Thomas Nast in *Harper's Weekly*. The most famous portrayed the Tammany Tiger snarling over the broken bodies of liberty and justice in a Roman arena presided over by Emperor Tweed and his gang. The public outcry led to a state investigation directed by Samuel Tilden that eventually sent most of the Tweed Ring to prison.

THE TAMMANY TIGER LOOSE, BY THOMAS NAST, HARPER'S WEEKLY, 1871
Cartoonist Thomas Nast invented the Tammany tiger as a vivid symbol of the Tweed gang's ruthlessness and rapacity. His trenchant drawings were widely credited with the overthrow of the corrupt Democratic administration in the fall of 1871.

Algernon Sydney emerged from the Tweed downfall without accusation of any wrongdoing. He had made such an outstanding reputation for himself as Assistant District Attorney that by the time he resigned in 1873 many thought he should be the next Democratic candidate for mayor. As an editorial in the *Evening Telegram* explained, "Although a prominent Tammanyite and an office-holder under the old regime, the name of Mr. Sullivan gathered luster. When almost every office-holder was charged with dishonesty or prosecuted for malfeasance…Mr. Sullivan stood so far above suspicion that even insinuation never whispered aught against him." Even the staunchly Republican *New-York Tribune* gave him begrudging praise: "With a general popularity among Democrats, he is, perhaps, as little exceptionable to the Republicans as any genuine member of the Democratic Party."

He steadfastly refused this and all other appeals to run for elective office. His uncertain health and the demands of his legal practice may have been factors, but his resistance ran deeper. Although he was indefatigable as an advocate for his principles and his clients, there was a central core of reticence in his character that made him quite incapable of promoting himself.

He did accept one other public office, but not for his own benefit. He was appointed in 1875 as Public Administrator, supervising the estates of people who died without leaving a will. He took the job, he explained to a friend, mainly to help an older colleague in financial straits – "to provide a place for Mr. Winder, who is a most competent and worthy man."

Although the position was only part time, he tackled it with his usual zeal. During his ten-year term, he reformed the office, replacing political appointees with able professionals, and was able to reduce the service fees charged to settle estates. "The books are clearly and accurately kept," reported the official auditors. "The accounts are in perfect order….We think we are justified in saying that the business has been economically administered."

Mary Mildred and the Nursery and Child's Hospital

From the 1870s on, as her son George grew up and his recurrent health problems required less of her personal attention, Mary Mildred was able to devote herself more fully to the volunteer work that she evidently loved. She concentrated most of her time and energy on the Nursery and Child's Hospital, whose board of directors she had joined in 1866.

NURSERY AND CHILD'S HOSPITAL, 51ST STREET AND LEXINGTON AVENUE
This major charitable institution was run entirely by women. Mary Mildred was an active member of its board of trustees from 1866, and would rise to become its chief officer, the First Directress, and to lead its fundraising efforts.
(New York Public Library Picture Collection)

She served the organization in several different capacities, starting with recording secretary. In this period, it was not acceptable for married women in polite society to work for pay, but there was no limit on what they could accomplish as volunteers. The Nursery and Child's Hospital was in fact run entirely by women, and its officers, from the First Directress down, were responsible for the day-to-day operations of its hospital, day-care center, and orphanage.

As a board member, Mary Mildred served on a committee making weekly visits to the Manhattan institution. When she was later elected Second Directress, she visited almost every day and spent one twelve-hour day each week traveling to the Staten Island branch. In short, she was working virtually full time, in demanding, high-responsibility positions.

The Nursery and Child's Hospital was supported financially by board members and other donors, but it also depended on one main fundraiser, the annual Charity Ball. This gala event was attended by the city's political leaders and most affluent citizens. It netted many thousands of dollars for the organization and also helped to bring public attention to its vital mission. In the early 1880s, interest in the event appeared to be flagging, and Mary Mildred volunteered to take charge. She became president of the Charity Ball in 1883, rejuvenated it, and continued to lead it for more than three decades.

Mary Mildred was widely acknowledged as a superb fundraiser. Unlike some other society leaders, she did not have enough wealth to inspire donors by her own giving. Through her personal charm and infectious enthusiasm, she was enormously effective in encouraging others to be generous and to reach out to friends and colleagues for further support.

Algernon Sydney's Later Years

Algernon Sydney's legal practice prospered quickly after the end of the Civil War. In 1870, he decided to expand by forming a partnership,

Sullivan, Kobbe, and Fowler, which lasted until 1878. The next year he founded a new partnership with a young protégé, 25-year-old William Nelson Cromwell. Cromwell had been hired in 1874 as an accountant at the former firm and Algernon Sydney found the young man so promising that he arranged to have him attend Columbia University Law School.

Sullivan and Cromwell added ten more lawyers over the next few years and it became one of the leading law firms in the city. Now the firm has some 800 lawyers in 12 offices around the world, and it is still a leader in its field.

George Hammond Sullivan joined Sullivan and Cromwell in 1885, after he himself had graduated from Columbia Law School. He remained a partner for the rest of his career.

Algernon Sydney was an accomplished and widely respected attorney. One colleague described him as "one of the strongest, readiest, and most successful jury lawyers at the Bar." A justice of the Court of Common Pleas wrote of him, "He was always welcomed by the Court in any case in which he appeared because it was felt that his learning, ability and absolute truthfulness would assist the Court in the trial of any question of law and fact with which it had to deal."

However, although he achieved moderate prosperity from his profession, he never became wealthy. He didn't limit his practice to affluent clients. On the contrary, he often took the cases of those who could pay him little or nothing but whose cause he thought was just. He avoided dunning clients for his fees and refused to prosecute those who defrauded him by paying with bad checks or worthless securities. Although he was a powerful and effective advocate in the courtroom, he was at heart a conciliator. "I can assure you," he told a friend, "that I compose twenty, thirty, yes forty causes of strife and discord where I now try one case."

Algernon Sydney was always generous in encouraging younger lawyers and newcomers to the profession. As one colleague later recalled, "No small part of my success is due to the good words and kind offices of Mr. Sullivan at the outset of my career." In 1872, he agreed to serve as vice president of the declining Arcadian Society, a social organization for young professionals in law, journalism, and the arts. He revived the group by making it the host of popular receptions for notable public figures, such as the Arctic explorer Isaac Hayes and Peter Cooper, founder of Cooper Union.

In 1880, Algernon Sydney sponsored former slave John H. Quarles as the first black member of the New York Bar. Racism was prevalent in this period, in the North as well as the South. Algernon Sydney's forthright statement of support demonstrated not only his personal lack of bias but also his opposition to injustice of any sort.

Outwardly, Algernon Sydney's demeanor was almost always calm and self-possessed. He was never known to lose his temper. Inwardly, however, there was a more sensitive and nervous side to his personality that would on occasion reveal itself. He suffered from insomnia. He would soothe his mind by walking over to the Hudson River and taking the ferry back and forth between Manhattan and New Jersey for hours before dawn.

He also found solace from the inevitable stresses of work in the simple habits of home life. He had a favorite hymn, "Art Thou Weary, Art Thou Languid?" that he would play on the piano when he returned each evening from the office. The rest of the household always knew he had arrived home when the familiar melody drifted from the parlor.

Able lawyer that he was, he never concealed the fact that he found more satisfaction in his volunteer activities than in his profession. He was able to devote more time to these matters once Sullivan and Cromwell became established and he could share more of his legal responsibilities with his colleagues. He served as an officer for many organizations, among them the New York College of Music, Presbyterian Hospital, the American Numismatic Society, and the committee for the design of the monument of the Battle of Saratoga. He was a loyal member of the Brick Presbyterian Church during his early years in New York and of the First Presbyterian Church when he settled on 11th Street. He taught Sunday school at both institutions, and founded the Young People's Association at First Presbyterian.

ALGERNON SYDNEY SULLIVAN IN 1879
When he was 53, Algernon Sydney founded Sullivan and Cromwell, which has grown
to become one of the most prominent law firms in the country.

His gifts as a public speaker were in constant demand and he seldom turned down a request. He spoke at the unveiling of a statue of General George Custer at West Point in 1879, at the erection of the monumental Egyptian obelisk known as Cleopatra's Needle in Central Park in 1880, and at the dedication of a bust of Edgar Allen Poe at the Metropolitan Museum of Art in 1885. He addressed innumerable commemorations, celebrations, and banquets. When a cornerstone was to be laid for the New York Produce Exchange in 1882, he managed to prepare and deliver a finely polished speech with just one hour's notice, after the scheduled speaker suddenly fell sick.

He remained a dedicated Democrat all his life, and a reliable campaigner for the party's presidential candidates. He delivered impassioned speeches for Samuel Tilden in 1876, for Winfield Scott in 1880, and (more successfully) for Grover Cleveland in 1884.

The New York Southern Society

On Washington's Birthday, February 22, 1887, Algernon Sydney spoke at a dinner celebrating the first anniversary of the New York Southern Society. This organization was founded by a group of Southern businessmen and professionals in New York, many of whom Algernon Sydney had befriended and encouraged when they first came to the city. Its mission was to heal the breach between North and South caused by the Civil War, and it was natural and appropriate for the founders to elect Algernon Sydney as the first president.

His address began with heartfelt praise for the end of hostility between the sections:

> It is twenty-two years since war ended between the Union and
> the Confederacy, and now we have perfect peace. Indeed, there
> is almost rivalry in a common patriotic enthusiasm between

these recent foes. Even the ashes from once-glowing embers have been scattered by the merciful winds, and we find not a spark of burnings or hate….We meet as the Southern Society of New York. We are not only in it, we are of it in deed and in very spirit.

He concluded with a list of several ideals that the society should aspire to. One of these ideals embodied more of a hope for the future than the reality of the period. It was to "care for and uphold those of our fellow citizens, without distinction of race, whose lot is affected by any burdens of the past."

The Death of Algernon Sydney Sullivan

Algernon Sydney's health had never been robust, and all his life he suffered from several debilitating illnesses. In late November, 1887, he came down with what at first seemed only a severe cold. However, it then developed into pneumonia, which in those days was often fatal. He died on December 4, 1887, at the age of 61.

The reaction to Algernon Sydney's death was immediate and virtually unanimous. Tributes appeared the next day in almost every New York newspaper. The *New York Times* summed up these widely shared sentiments with particular force:

> The announcement that Algernon Sydney Sullivan is dead will prove a great shock and a cause of honest regret not only to his friends and acquaintances, who are many, but to the public at large, for he was looked upon as a man of great ability, of a kindness of heart that could not be measured, of never-ending desire to promote such projects as were for the benefit of the people, and more than all, he was considered a politician who was absolutely pure.

The *New York Herald* offered a vivid personal description:

> He was known far and wide as a gifted orator, and his tall, spare
> figure was familiar to most New Yorkers. His strong, clear-cut
> features, his gleaming dark eyes, his short, snow-white mus-
> tache, his large head fringed with closely cropped white hair,
> and his scrupulous neatness of attire were known to nearly
> everybody in this city. His manner was ordinarily mild and af-
> fable and his words slow, polite, and very distinct.

The *New York World* also provided a revealing personal detail:

> Down town the feeling of sorrow was widespread….A waiter in
> the Astor House paid him a tribute, saying, "He was a great
> enough man to be able to treat those below him with respect."

Journals as distant as the *New Orleans Picayune* soon offered similar
praises:

> A leading lawyer, a leading Democrat, a leading club man, a
> leader in society – all these and more was Mr. Sullivan. He was
> one of the silver-tongued of his generation….In every depart-
> ment of life he seemed to have interest and insight. He was one
> of those [whom] New Yorkers like to point out as representative
> citizens. There is none to fill the vacancy he left in the ranks.

Memorials in his honor were issued by many of the organizations and institutions with which he was associated. In the extensive memorial from
the Southern Society, a long-time friend offered an assessment that would
undoubtedly have pleased him:

> I knew his father, in Madison, Indiana….He was a man univer-

sally beloved, who respected the simple Christian life and character, who died lamented by the whole community. The son followed the example of the father.

In a letter of condolence to Mary Mildred, Algernon Sydney's partner and protégé, William Nelson Cromwell, coined the phrase that has summed up Algernon Sydney Sullivan's character ever since. He was, Cromwell wrote, "always gracious and altogether loveable; putting aside, not putting forward, his own great personality; reaching out both hands in constant helpfulness to men."

Three years later, a group of friends, associates, and admirers formed the Algernon Sydney Sullivan Memorial Committee to assure that his achievements and character would not be forgotten. Its 77 members included former president Grover Cleveland, railroad executive Chauncey Depew, philanthropist Elbridge Gerry, author Edward Everett Hale, artists Albert Bierstadt and George Inness, university president Seth Low, inventor and industrialist Cyrus H. McCormick, and Civil War hero Horace Porter – to name just a few.

Over the next three-and-a-half decades the committee would sponsor several projects in Algernon Sydney's honor. The first was a public drinking fountain bearing his portrait, erected at Van Cortlandt Park in 1906. The following year, a bronze portrait bust was given to the New York headquarters of Alpha Delta Phi, the fraternity to which Algernon Sydney had belonged as a student at Miami University. In 1909, a memorial plaque was commissioned and casts were presented to New York Law schools and other civic institutions. Later, the committee would initiate an even more far-reaching form of commemoration, the Algernon Sydney Sullivan Awards, described in detail in the following sections.

Mary Mildred's Bereavement

Mary Mildred was devastated by the loss of the husband she had loved and admired for almost 32 years. One friend reported, "It was only the strength of a disciplined will" that enabled her to get through the funeral service. In a photograph taken about this time, she is shown dressed in mourning, her eyes downcast, her expression conveying both sorrow and resignation. Like many widows of the time, she wore black for the rest of her life.

MARY MILDRED SULLIVAN IN 1888
In a photograph taken shortly after Algernon Sydney's death, Mary Mildred is shown dressed in full mourning. Like many widows of the time, she wore black for the rest of her life.

Then and after, she was strengthened by the steadfast support of George, who had just turned 28 when his father died. George was an attorney with Sullivan and Cromwell. He was living at the family home on 11th Street and remained there for the rest of his mother's life and his own.

Mary Mildred found solace in her charitable work, especially for the Nursery and Child's Hospital. She was elected as its top officer, or First Directress, in 1888, and continued to serve as president of the Charity Ball, as she had since 1883. George not only was her chief assistant, but also as the years passed would take on more and more of the responsibilities for this demanding but crucially lucrative event.

A Renewed Interest in Southern Welfare

Ever since Mary Mildred had served on the New York Ladies Relief Association, which raised money to aid Southern victims of the Civil War, she remained concerned for the welfare of the region where she had grown up and where most of her family lived. During the three decades after the 1860s, her charitable efforts were primarily concentrated on organizations in New York, particularly the Nursery and Child's Hospital. Toward the end of the century, however, her attention returned to the land she still considered home.

The United Daughters of the Confederacy was one of several societies that sprang up in the 1890s. Mary Mildred joined the New York chapter soon after the organization was founded in 1894. She was not especially interested in some of the principal goals of the organization, such as preserving the memories of Confederate veterans and building memorials in their honor. Neither did she engage in the society's defense of the so-called "Lost Cause" interpretation of history, which maintained that the Civil War was primarily a conflict over states' rights rather than slavery. Rather, Mary Mildred saw in the society an opportunity for Southern women to become empowered, so that they could improve not only their own economic and social condition but also the education and well-being of their children.

Mary Mildred became an active member of the society and utilized its meetings to advocate support of Southern schools. She was also very effective in raising money for the organization. In 1912, a second chapter was formed in New York; it was named the Mary Mildred Sullivan Chapter in her honor, and she served as its first president. In her report at the society's annual meeting, she reiterated her conviction that philanthropy in general and aid to education in particular should be central elements of the society's mission in the South. She cited the example, almost fifty years earlier, of the New York Ladies Relief Association in aiding Southern victims of the Civil War.

The Southern Industrial Education Association

Martha Sawyer Gielow, like Mary Mildred, was a Southern-born woman who lived in the North. She separated from her husband in the 1890s and made her home with her two children in New York. She created a successful career for herself by writing and performing songs and stories drawn from her childhood in rural Alabama. She was also devoted to improving education in her native region, particularly the neglected and impoverished mountain country of Appalachia.

In 1905, Mrs. Gielow became one of the founders of the Southern Industrial Educational Association. Its mission was to aid so-called industrial schools, which provided basic education in areas where public schools were virtually nonexistent. Subsidized by donations and volunteer staff, industrial schools charged little or no tuition and usually included work-study programs that taught students practical skills and generated products ranging from food to furniture, either to be used at the schools or sold outside. The schools served as community centers and became involved in the revival of traditional arts and crafts, such as weaving, woodworking, quilt-making, and basketry, which became increasingly popular in the early twentieth century. They also contributed to the preservation and dissemination of folk music, folk art, and traditional storytelling.

MARY MILDRED AND GEORGE HAMMOND SULLIVAN IN 1906
George Sullivan faithfully and capably assisted his mother in many of her charitable activities, and often served as her surrogate in organizations such as the Nursery and Child's Hospital and the Southern Industrial Education Association.

On April 7, 1906, Mrs. Gielow gave a recital of Southern songs and stories to a small but select audience at the Astor Hotel in New York. Among those who attended was Mary Mildred. After the performance,

Mrs. Gielow took her aside and asked for her support for the recently formed association. Mary Mildred probably didn't need much persuading for her to organize a New York auxiliary of the organization and to serve as its president. She mildly protested that at the age of 69 she was too old for the task, "but if my Southland needs me, I am at her service."

Drawing upon her broad network of charitable donors, Mary Mildred quickly built the New York auxiliary into the most successful in the association – it consistently raised more money than the rest combined. With George's faithful assistance, and using the model of the Charity Balls for the Nursery and Children's Hospital, she organized annual Mardi Gras Balls that became the auxiliary's most important fundraising events.

Mary Mildred's and George's work for the Southern Industrial Education Association was to have significant consequences later on. It focused their attention upon the special needs of Appalachia, and upon the importance of education in improving the well-being and future progress of its people.

Donations of Art
and Other Philanthropies

In the early 1900s, while recovering from one of his periodic illnesses, George Sullivan began visiting art galleries, antique shops, and book dealers. On behalf of his mother and himself, he assembled a large collection of prints and other works of art, rare books, and historical documents. But they soon began disbursing their holdings in gifts to colleges and libraries. Their first major donation was to the George Peabody College for Teachers (now part of Vanderbilt University) in Nashville, Tennessee. Mary Mildred had become friendly with a graduate of the college, Mrs. Francis Edwards Hill in 1912 and learned from Mrs. Hill that the art teachers there were in great need of a study collection. She and George agreed that, in George's words, "we had found a splendid outlet for our desire to aid students."

Using the United Daughters of the Confederacy as their agent, they began donating prints and other works of art that eventually totaled some 10,000 items.

In following years they made other generous offerings. They owned a collection of George Washington memorabilia that went to the Mount Vernon Association. The University of Maryland and George Washington University received historical documents concerning their origins. The New-York Historical Society was presented with a large collection of books, including Francis Scott Key's law library. The New York Public Library and the Brooklyn Museum were given multitudes of prints – 3,000 to the library and 8,000 to the museum.

George Sullivan formally retired from Sullivan and Cromwell in 1913 at the relatively young age of 53. He cited his declining health as the primary reason– like his father, he often suffered from infections and other ailments. But he may also have wanted to devote more time to his own personal interests and to assisting Mary Mildred in her wide-ranging charitable activities.

Mary Mildred never lost her unfaltering devotion to helping others, but as she entered her eighties, her physical energies began to wane. When the United States entered World War I, she became a leader in the Southern Women's Patriotic Committee of New York. Its 300 members worked in hospitals, sold Liberty Bonds, and raised money for the Red Cross. Shortly after the Armistice in November 1918, Mary Mildred suffered a temporary physical breakdown, possibly a mild attack of the epidemic influenza brought on, at least in part, by overexertion.

In 1919, Mary Mildred retired from all her duties at the Nursery and Child's Hospital, which she had served for more than half a century. She nonetheless continued her association with such organizations as the United Daughters of the Confederacy and the Southern Industrial Education Association.

MARY MILDRED SULLIVAN IN 1924, AT AGE 88
After her retirement from the Nursery and Children's Hospital in 1919, Mary Mildred
continued to participate in several of her other charitable activities.

The Algernon Sydney Sullivan Awards

The remaining members of the Algernon Sydney Sullivan Memorial Committee, founded in 1890, decided by 1925 to conclude their work with one final project in honor of Algernon Sydney. They collaborated with the Southern Society of New York to co-sponsor awards in the form of commemorative plaques bearing Algernon Sydney's portrait to be presented at Southern colleges and universities to deserving individuals for "excellence of character and service to humanity." It may well have been George and his mother who suggested that the first institution to present the Algernon Sydney Sullivan Awards should be the George Peabody College in Nashville, with which they had formed a warm personal relationship.

A year later, the Memorial Committee formally dissolved, and the Southern Society became the sole sponsor. The Algernon Sydney Sullivan Awards program was expanded to fifteen colleges and universities, most of them in Appalachia. Annual awards were typically presented to an outstanding senior student and sometimes to an alumnus or a member of the community who had significantly aided the institution. The program continued to grow over the years, and Algernon Sydney Sullivan Awards came to be among the most prestigious prizes offered in Southern higher education.

The Algernon Sydney Sullivan Awards were presented mainly though not exclusively to men. In 1940, the United Daughters of the Confederacy established Mary Mildred Sullivan Awards for women. Offered at women's colleges and coeducational colleges and universities, these, too, have become widely adopted and highly prized.

ALGERNON SYDNEY SULLIVAN AWARDS MEDALLION

The Algernon Sydney Sullivan Foundation now administers both the Algernon Sydney Sullivan Awards, originally created by the Southern Society, and the Mary Mildred Sullivan Awards, created by the United Daughters of the Confederacy.

GEORGE HAMMOND SULLIVAN IN 1934, AT AGE 74
After his mother's death in 1933, George Sullivan became primarily responsible for
focusing the Algernon Sydney Sullivan Foundation's mission upon the improvement of
education in the South.

George Sullivan and Rollins College

Among the first colleges to offer the Algernon Sydney Sullivan Awards, beginning in 1927, was an institution outside Appalachia – Rollins College, in Winter Park, Florida. Always coeducational, Rollins is one of the institutions that receives funds from the Algernon Sydney Sullivan Foundation and presents Algernon Sydney Sullivan Awards to both male and female graduating seniors, as well as occasionally to deserving local community members. George Sullivan took an interest in Rollins and became friends with its eighth president, Hamilton Holt, an internationally renowned journalist, social activist, politician, and pacifist who served as Rollins' president for 24 years (1925-1949). Over the years, Rollins became one of George's favorite philanthropies, and he made substantial donations to the college.

In 1936, the same year in which the Algernon Sydney Sullivan Foundation began supporting the Sullivan Scholars Program at Rollins, George began giving the college works of art and other pieces from his parents' estate. In 1940, Irving Bachellor, the distinguished novelist and honorary Rollins trustee who received the college's initial Algernon Sydney Sullivan Award in 1927, presented George Sullivan with the Rollins College Decoration of Honor. In 1947, George made a gift to Rollins that enabled the college to name a facility on campus in memory of his parents and Sullivan Memorial House was dedicated the following year. It served for many years as a home for meetings and services of Rollins' Circle of Sullivan Scholars, as well as for meetings of other student service organizations and initiatives at the college. For a time it also housed memorabilia of the Sullivan family. In the late 1990s, Rollins began using Sullivan House as a classroom, and it remains a popular and well-used classroom today.

The Last Years of Mary Mildred Sullivan

After her retirement from the Nursery and Child's Hospital, Mary Mildred continued to participate in her other charitable activities. She attended meetings of the United Daughters of the Confederacy and continued to press for aid to Southern education. She remained involved with the New York auxiliary of the Southern Industrial Education Association and its annual Mardi Gras Balls. As president emeritus of the auxiliary, she helped with the dissolution of the organization in 1926, and with a transfer of the auxiliary's remaining funds to a similar organization, the Educational and Relief Fund for Southern Mountaineers.

She depended more and more upon George, who served as her substitute and representative on charity committees and managed her wide-ranging philanthropic donations. Her reliance upon him became even more intense in 1929, when she fell and broke a hip, an accident from which she never fully recovered. She was largely confined to the upper floor of their home for the rest of her life, and George spent most of his time taking care of her.

Mary Mildred Sullivan died on June 9, 1933, at the age of 96. In accordance with her wishes, George had her body transported to Virginia, where she was buried with other members of her family at Mount Hebron Cemetery in Winchester.

The Algernon Sydney Sullivan Foundation

As early as 1924, Mary Mildred and George began planning for a memorial to Algernon Sydney that would endure after their own lifetimes. They consulted with a cousin of Mary Mildred's, David Milton, and with William E. Bardusch, their attorney and a partner at Sullivan and

Cromwell. They concluded that the most effective solution would be to form a charitable foundation, which they could endow, and which would be empowered to make grants to worthwhile institutions and individuals. There are many thousands of such foundations today, but at that time they were still relatively rare – no more than about 300 of them existed in the country.

The Sullivans requested a charter for the foundation from the New York State Legislature in late 1929. The charter was issued on March 30, 1930. The basic mission of the foundation was stated in fairly general terms. Its purpose was to promote

> the welfare of mankind…and to continue, carry out and further
> the philanthropies and philanthropic aims of the late Algernon
> Sydney Sullivan and Mary Mildred Sullivan, and more particu-
> larly to contribute funds for the support, education, maintenance,
> care and training of children of any age and circumstance.

But the charter also described some of the specific functions of the foundation. It would, for example, present scholarships, awards, and prizes to teachers and students in colleges and universities "for excellence in character, service to humanity, scholarship or other activities," as well as to alumni for "conspicuous and meritorious service to humanity of any nature."

The foundation did not become active right away because George was occupied with caring for his mother in her last years. The first meeting of the trustees took place on June 27, 1934. William Bardusch was elected president, and George vice president. Founding gifts were recorded in the meeting minutes— $10,000 from Mary Mildred Sullivan and $500 from George Sullivan.

The following November, the foundation issued its first two grants. Rollins College was given $85 for prize essays about the life of Algernon Sydney Sullivan, and George Peabody College received $200 for four student scholarships.

George Sullivan then became primarily responsible for sharpening the focus of the foundation. First of all, it would concentrate upon educational institutions in and near Appalachia – the region to which Mary Mildred had devoted so much love and effort as a leader of the Southern Industrial Education Association. Almost all of these institutions would be colleges and universities, where students would prepare for their roles as adults. Most of the institutions would be relatively small, with many of their students in need of financial aid. Finally, the grants from the foundation, while funneled through these institutions, would be earmarked for scholarships and other forms of direct student aid. These guidelines have shaped the mission of the foundation ever since.

The Last Years of George Hammond Sullivan

Although he had suffered from poor health periodically since early childhood, George Sullivan lived to a great age. He continued to make his home at 16 West 11th Street, the house where he had grown up, spending his last years in quiet retirement. He died on November 15, 1956, just a few days short of his 97th birthday. The chapel bell at Rollins College rang 97 times in his honor.

Conclusion: the Sullivan Legacy

The Algernon Sydney Sullivan Foundation continues to support higher education in the South through scholarships and grants. Its resources have multiplied far beyond the original gifts and bequests of its founders, and in recent years, it has expanded its reach beyond Appalachia to several other colleges and universities in the Southeastern states. The foundation now supervises the Algernon Sydney Sullivan Awards, originally created by the Southern Society, and the Mary Mildred Sullivan Awards, created by the United Daughters of the Confederacy. The mission of the foundation remains essentially the same: to inspire young people to lead lives of integrity, characterized by service to their communities.

Recently the Sullivan Foundation connected its founding vision to the present day through its Service and Social Entrepreneurship Program. This forward-looking mission for the Foundation seeks to advance the already steady momentum of social entrepreneurship, which stands as one of the most exciting developments in social change for the current generation. In short, social entrepreneurs apply self-sustaining business principles to influence social change within a community.

In 2010, the Foundation established its first Service and Social Entrepreneurship Fall Retreat Weekend, which brought together Sullivan school students, faculty, and staff with active social entrepreneurs for a weekend of mentoring and business planning. Since this first weekend, the Foundation has continued to hold retreat weekends once a semester and has seen the attendance and interest grow.

Also in 2010, the Foundation held its first Sullivan Summer Institute in Social Entrepreneurship at Sewanee: The University of the South. Since 2010 the college course offerings in the Sullivan Summer Institute have grown and are presently taught in several locations around the world each summer.

The Foundation has also been working with individual schools and faculty to help educate and promote new and creative solutions to our community's social problems. In addition to the continuation of the retreat weekend and summer institute programs, the Sullivan Foundation Service & Social Entrepreneurship Program continues to explore new ways in which to support schools interested in social entrepreneurship, including campus engagement, curriculum development, and social business plan competitions.

Participants in the Service & Social Entrepreneurship Program have gone on to found a wide array of socially conscious business ventures in both domestic and international markets. Many of our schools have adopted a social entrepreneurship minor or major, or have incorporated these concepts into extra-curricular programs. In doing so, the Sullivan Foundation remains as relevant to today's social climate as the one in which it began.

MARY MILDRED SULLIVAN AWARDS MEDALLION
In 1940, the United Daughters of the Confederacy established the Mary Mildred Sullivan Awards for women, corresponding to the Algernon Sydney Sullivan Awards presented mainly to men. Both are now administered by the Algernon Sydney Sullivan Foundation.

Made in the USA
Columbia, SC
12 January 2019